SUMMARY

OF

THE SECRET BOOK OF

FLORA LEA : A Novel

(A Guide To Patti Callahan Henry's Book)

Jessica Looney

TABLE Of CONTENTS

DISCLAIMER

You are reading the summary of the book "THE SECRET BOOK OF FLORA LEA " .

This summary's information is not prepared to take the place of the original book. It serves as a summary to deepen the reader's comprehension .

Once again the goal of this summary book is to persuade readers to purchase the original work in order to deepen their grasp .

Copyright © Jessica Looney 2023 .

CHAPTER ONE

Flora Lea Linden is six years old and wakes alone on a scarlet blanket by the River Thames. She stares over the verdant expanse, at the churning water of the River Thames wrinkled with winks and puckers as it almost over ows its banks. She stares over the verdant expanse, at the churning water of the River Thames wrinkled with winks and puckers as it almost over ows its banks. She stares over the verdant expanse, at the churning water of the River Thames wrinkled with winks and puckers as it almost over ows its banks. She stares over the verdant expanse, at the churning water of the River Thames wrinkled with winks and puckers as it almost over ows its banks.

She stares over the verdant expanse, at the churning water of the River Thames wrinkled with winks and puckers as it almost over ows its banks. She stares around the lush expanse, at the churning water of the River Flora is a magnificent, starry river that has been outlawed by Hazel. She clings on Berry by his worn, hairy paw and advances close to the water's surge, exhilarated at her daring. She hears a voice close in the woods, familiar, but ignores it.

The river is Flora's companion, her buddy, and this familiarity has her sliding progressively closer to its brink.

Hazel has chosen today that Flora will be a rabbit, and Flora peers down at the river's churned-up waters, seeking for stars but seeing only muck and silt. She slides down on a muddy, dirt gradient, landing on her bottom. Berry falls from her fingers as her hands and ngers dig into the moist dirt to save herself from sliding into the icy river. She scoots closer, hoping to grasp Berry, but he is too near to the water. She reaches for his paw, echoing her sister's words: "It's okay, it'

Hazel Linden's last day at Bloomsbury's Hogan's Rare Book Shoppe was like any other weekday spent arranging, classifying, and safeguarding the extraordinary stock of the shop. She took in every element of her last workday with a touch of sorrow and theatrical flair. She saw everything from behind the old cash register while wearing a brand-new Mary Quant knockoff that she had purchased at the Notting Hill street market. They all sought the position at Sotheby's where she now works, but Hazel was picked. Hazel is departing from Hogan's to work with Lord Arthur Dickson at Sotheby's.

She has conflicting emotions about the transfer since it would mean leaving behind the security and comfort of the store and her coworkers, Edwin Hogan and his son Tim. The youngest of them, Poppy, has been employed there since she turned 18; Edwin had previously advised her to either start working there or quit. Hazel learns afterwards that Poppy has nowhere else to go. Poppy was a military orphan who had been trying to find work, but no one would take a risk on her. She was given a new lease on life by Edwin, who also showed her how to inspire a customer's passion for rare books.

With four other women, she now shares a two-bedroom flat and dreams of the future. She was thrilled when Edwin asked her to process fresh arrivals and put them in the safe since Sotheby's is the biggest auction house in the world. For fifteen years, Hazel has been a bookseller for Edwin. She has an innate ability to find intriguing books before anybody else is aware that they are accessible. Two columns in Hazel's logbook—quality and ID number—are designated for her personal entries.

She gives each item that enters via the back door an inventory number, records its condition, and stores it in the safe until Edwin determines where and how to exhibit it.

She also appreciates each book for its history, including who owned, cherished, and passed it along. The most crucial information in this passage is that Hazel and Barnaby have planned a week-long vacation to Paris and that Hazel has saved her pennies and pounds for two new clothes for the occasion. She is welcomed by a tall guy wearing a black felt hat and an overcoat that is almost completely covered with raindrops, as well as a lady with raven hair. He informs her that he is searching for her when she asks whether she can assist.

Edwin and Hazel get together at Foyles to get a copy of the privately produced Auden poetry from 1928. Tim rearranges a shelf of children's books as Edwin goes on an errand and Hazel quotes Auden with a grin. Tim is rearranging a shelf of children's books while Edwin performs errands.

In Bloomsbury, England, Hazel and Flora waited in their backyard for their mother to return from her shift at the Royal Voluntary Service. Hazel envisioned bombs dropping on her, her sister, her home, and her mother as she viewed black-and-white film of warplanes in the skies at school. Although she wanted to be courageous, the idea of leaving Bloomsbury and Mecklenburgh Square and their two-bedroom apartment made her uneasy and prevented her from getting any rest.

CHAPTER TWO

She didn't get why moving somewhere would be so important if bombs finally dropped from the sky. Although Papa had advised Hazel and Flora to reserve their inquiries for class, they were too old to be treated in that manner.

Hazel felt jealous of her younger sister as Papa kissed her on the forehead. Before giving Flora to Mum, Papa yanked her arms away from his neck and kissed her cheeks. Hazel hoped that one day a guy will see her the same way after Papa made a commitment to return to his daughters. Papa, who passed away a year ago owing to an unreliable engine during RAF training, is joined by Hazel, Mum, and Flora as they stand in the backyard garden. Until Papa comes back, they act as if nothing is wrong, but a week later a telegram informs them that he has passed away.

They are terrified by them despite the fact that Flora's red and blue and Hazel's dark black Mickey Mouse masks don't function. Hazel tells her sister a tale about her grandmother, who had a birthmark similar to her own and received it from an ancestor. The fact that Hazel is left with her sister Flora and is left to come up with fresh tales to help her overcome her anxiety is one of the most crucial points in this novel. She informs Flora that they may travel to an unseen location that is just outside of them. Flora informs Hazel that there are hidden gates that are only accessible to the deserving, and that if they are deserving, they may enter them.

Then, Hazel informs Flora that if she is deserving, she may enter the secret gateways that are concealed under the rocks. Flora and Hazel, two sisters, have discovered Whisperwood and the River of Stars, a beautiful place where they are free to be whomever or whatever they want. Whisperwood and the River of Stars is the name of their new home, and they have been given names that honor both flora and their mother, Camellia. The kingdom, which is formed of owers, rivers, and trees much like them, excites Hazel and Flora, who are eager to visit and explore it. If they don't get lost, they must come back here.

Sisters Flora and Hazel are destined to be the same thing, but they aren't aware of it yet. They enter the woodland by speaking its name three times, as Hazel assures Flora there is always an owl looking over them. Hazel leads them through woodlands with branches so large and strong they seem to be able to support them as Flora grinned and raised her arms.

In their made-up country, Flora and Hazel see comets and stars. When their mother calls, dressed in a pink and yellow outfit with long golden hair, they are terrified.

She holds a piece of cream-colored paper in her palm, her mouth is twisted, and her eyes are attentive. The plot centers on Hazel and Flora, twin orphans who flee the Shire Orphanage's harshness and find the Kingdom of Whisperwood, where they may transform into anyone or whatever they choose. After 20 years of looking for her sister, Hazel discovers a clue in the book Whisperwood by American author Peggy Andrews, who lives in Massachusetts and is chronicling her own life. Hazel is adamant on finding Flora, but she is unsure whether she will be successful or if she will ever see her sister again. Though she is adamant on finding Flora, she is unsure of when she will see her again.

When Hazel hears a jingling sound coming from the kitchen wall, she understands it is the telephone there. Tim greets her with a "Hallo" and she removes the green plastic receiver from its cradle. He enquired as to her well-being while seeming apprehensive. Having had a late night, Hazel feels apologetic for departing without saying goodbye. He agrees to share information about her first day at Sotheby's with everyone and makes a commitment to do so.

She is hesitant to apologize to him and admit what she had done. The most crucial information in this passage is that Hazel took a package out the back door, promised to return it the next day, and made the decision to jot down every potential scenario for how this book may have been authored by an American author and then ended up at Hogan's Rare Book Shop. A robin's egg-colored notepad was taken from the bottom shelf of the wood hutch that was opened on the opposite wall of the kitchen. She set the drawings in a pile at the far side of the table after picking up her beloved silver engraved nib pen and green clay inkpot. She opened to the first unlined blank page, her pen hesitating as an ink-tear slid to the white paper, and saw the top drawing, which matched the book's cover. She then made an effort to recall who had been there when Flora and she had shared the tale in a whisper, but it was impossible to be nice.

On a kitchen counter, Barnaby and Hazel are seated next to one another. Barnaby gestures toward a collection of sketches that Hazel stole from the store. Even though she shudders at the thought of returning them, she decides to do so.

They talk about Peggy Andrews, the book, the plot, and how and why it came to be. From his pocket, Barnaby yanks out a crimson crumpled package of cigarettes.

Despite having been together for three years, Hazel and Barnaby are not yet prepared to be married. While Barnaby is hesitant to give up his work and his independence, Hazel is hesitant to give up her freedom and wants all that marriage and family entail. When Hazel marries again, he will get a sapphire-and-diamond ring that belonged to his grandmother in the past. After lighting up, Barnaby goes to get his highball, but the glass topples, sending an amber river over the table. While Barnaby took a tea towel from her mother that had a cross-stitched map of London on it, Hazel grabbed a stack of drawings off the kitchen sink.

Hazel knelt down to inspect them after they clashed during their frenzied maneuvers. She discovered a stone home with smoke curling from the chimney, flower-filled window boxes, and a blotch of amber-colored whiskey in the corner. With two ruined drawings in their hands and holding them guilty, Barnaby and Hazel remain still. Barnaby arrives at the door and informs Hazel that while Edwin loves her, he really loves his antiquities and rare book collection more.

Hazel must decide whether to leave the house, hand the package to the authorities, and claim it was an error—or hide the drawings at the back of the hutch where a hidden door concealed crucial family documents.

The most crucial information in this passage is that Hazel and Barnaby first meet in the living room, where Hazel is concerned about a barking dog that is preventing a little kid from going to sleep. Bobby is given a shoulder slap by Barnaby, who then leads him outside while closing the door and burying her face in her hands. After that, he kisses her, and they start to date. Hazel needs to erase the boundary between the past and the present since the past serves as an anchor for her. A memory box containing recollections of Flora, Oxford, the person who housed them, and Harry, the child she shared a residence with during the evacuation, had been forced open by Whisperwood.

Hazel got out of bed and looked in the mirror, thinking she may be attractive. Once the cigarette smoke seemed gone, she turned on the shower and scrubbed her hair till it was clean. Realizing what was at risk—arrest and losing her job at Sotheby's—she buckled her robe and crept into the living room. Only two of the twenty drawings were damaged, so she looked for answers.

Those who thought Flora's tale was finished came to mind, including Aiden Davies, who had made the call and said, "We believe we've found her." The remains of a corpse were discovered along the marshy bank of the River Thames on December 6, 1956, by a group of youths who had sneaked out under the full moon with a bottle of Jameson.

Flora's whereabouts were the subject of a beach search by Aiden Davies, who also left photographs and spoke with nearby residents. The remains of a corpse were discovered near the marshy border of the river on December 6th, 1956, by a group of youths who had sneaked out under the full moon with a bottle of Jameson. Both Hazel and Mum had left Aiden Davies, certain that this corpse did not explain Flora's enigma. Hazel would keep believing Flora had lived until there was evidence to the contrary. Hogan's Rare Book Shoppe in London employs bookseller Hazel Linden.

The author of her book, Peggy Andrews, is available for an interview. The guy requests that she send a letter to him at Henry-Todd Publishing's New York City address, along with the name of a publicist. When Hazel inquires as to Ms. Andrews' age, he replies that she will be 25 in April. Then he informs her that Flora would have been at least a year younger than Peggy Andrews, whose birthday is in July.

In order to learn more about her sister Flora, Hazel has to get in touch with the author of Whisperwood and The River of Stars.

In order to get a response from Peggy Andrews, she must be kind and persistent. She must compose a letter outlining the circumstances behind her sister's tale.

Outside the Oxford railway station, the banished kids made their way in a line while avoiding taxis and zebra crossings. They passed the stately steeples and college entrances of the city on their route. Hazel paused to glance at the lad who said, "Welcome to Oxford!" He waved frantically at all the kids walking by, but Hazel's bag shattered, and her things were all over the place. Hazel struggled vehemently against a person stooping over her and snatching up her brushes while Flora held the hem of her dress and rough and tender hands grabbed hold of her backpack.

At the town hall, where families choose which children to take home, Hazel and Flora arrive. Flora tugs at Hazel's hand and gestures toward their class, dispersing as she is being held firmly by Hazel. Hazel falls short of Flora, who sparkles like a diamond. Hazel falls short as the lady fixes her intense gaze on Flora. Hazel is chosen by Kelty Monroe, a young woman with auburn hair so vivid it almost appears on her.

CHAPTER THREE

Hazel and Flora were forced to flee a city that had been attacked. Locals choose them to stay in their houses as a billet, but Hazel and Flora are not. An image of a lady traversing ruins in a bombed-out city can be seen on a poster that is hanging on the wall. They each get a chocolate cookie and an enamel milk cup from a lady wearing a blue dirndl skirt. Sweat and wet wool can be smelled in the air as they eagerly consume food and drink.

The most crucial information in this passage is that Hazel and Flora are waiting for their mother to get home, and that a group of attractive women are approaching them while wearing brilliant blue dresses. Hazel Mersey Linden is who she introduces herself as while grinning at them. She invites them to meet her and grins at them. The woman laughs and makes the place smell like home; she has a nice smile and seems to be friends with their mother. Hazel and Flora make the decision to choose a guy to assist them.

Although Hazel's mother declined her wish to bring two daughters home, she was kind and gracious about it. Virginia Woolf was a member of the Bloomsbury Group and Flora was from Bloomsbury in London. The Bloomsbury Group captivated Harry's mother, who secretly wishes she had joined them. Harry didn't flinch when Hazel kissed him on the cheek. Two of the Linden family's children have come by train; they are Hazel Mersey and Flora Lea Linden.

An lovely youngster with an aura of innocence and sweetness, Flora Lea Linden is introduced to Bridgette Aberdeen and Hazel Mersey Linden. The two kids will be traveling home with them, Bridgette Aberdeen then gestures with her hand to the observer at the end of the bench.

Ash of light fills Hazel's Bloomsbury bedroom, and the phone is ringing. Edwin Hogan is phoning to see if she spotted anything strange since she is running late for work. She tells Edwin a fib, saying she left a package for Tim outside unattended, but Edwin is certain she did. Hazel discloses that she was able to get the original artwork for Baynes's book, which will be worth one penny once it is discovered in Britain. Hazel disputes Edwin's claim that she saw them after he made it.

The most crucial information in this passage is that Hazel was unhappy and emotional, and that Edwin left the home without reading through the documents. When Edwin questioned whether he could remember anybody who entered the rear room, Hazel bolted for the restroom. She went outdoors carrying a letter addressed to Peggy Andrews after discovering a message affixed to a wood panel. She remembered writing the postcard to Mum from Binsey that day as she read the letter, and she saw that the first half of the tale was accurate while the second was an inadvertent fabrication. Harry sat in the front passenger seat of Mrs. Aberdeen's blue Flying Nine as Hazel and Flora traveled.

The sky was low and dove gray outside, and the windshield was being loudly cleaned by the wipers. Mrs. Aberdeen sang a song about being "too marvelous for words" while she drove while holding the steering wheel in both hands. Flora remained silent as she gazed out the windows, and the dusk-colored surroundings nearly made her think that Whisperwood was conceivable. The automobile seemed as if it could collapse as they banged over a lengthy gravel road that was covered in so many ruts and dips.

The Aberdeen home is a charming stone building with a vivid blue front door and window boxes brimming with green leafy plants and red and yellow flowers when the sisters arrive.

The copper chimney pot is lit by the setting sun, and the roof is covered with black slate. Mrs. Aberdeen and Harry greet the sisters as they enter the home with their luggage. The inside has a substitute for the riverstone, a log-log fireplace, exposed beams, uneven plaster walls, and books on wooden side tables and shelves. Ivy on an arbor is woven into the pattern of the rug. Harry and Bridget Aberdeen reside at the Aberdeen cottage.

Mrs. Aberdeen welcomes Flora and Hazel to the cottage and gives them a warm welcome. In the foyer, Harry left his bags. Now he picks them up and takes them to the kitchen, where there is a brick fire, the red barn, and the vegetable garden with the willow cages. The cabinets are overflowing with dishes, mugs, glasses, and linens, while the worktops, AGA stove, and drapes are all covered in a deep shade of green. When Harry and Hazel go to the residence, they see a bed covered in blankets, a dark wood wardrobe, and a dresser covered in frilly lace.

They share a room with two windows that look out over the back fields, a dresser and wardrobe covered in frilly lace, and a bed.

Before supper, Harry beams and tells Flora a tale. Flora spins around the room's center while wearing her outfit. The room is filled with the noises of Mrs. Aberdeen's cooking, pottery banging, and wireless music. Guy Lombardo's song about September in the rain may be heard when Hazel and Flora survey the landscape. Mum's letter, which exhorts them to show bravery and look out for one another, was read by Hazel and Flora.

They will pay them a visit as soon as possible. Hazel is in charge of unpacking their luggage, and Flora instructs her to keep an eye out for one another. She folds her white shirt and owered dress before placing them on the dresser. Flora clings so closely that Hazel is unable to release her hold as she puts their coats and two matching blue dresses in the closet.

When Hazel enters Hogan's Rare Book Shoppe, she finds Tim and Edwin, two police inspectors hunched over a ledger at the long wood table. Hazel admits that she stole a package and left it in their path. Edwin becomes furious, becoming crimson, his bulbous nose turning yellow, and his eyes becoming rheumy.

Hazel rejects his suggestion to tell Chief Inspector Norman about the circumstance. Edwin's nose becomes yellow and his face goes crimson.

Former Edwin's employee Hazel Linden is charged with stealing a package from his business. Tim, Edwin's son, informs him that despite Hazel's hardships, she has no justification for her actions. The tallest of the two bobbies, a guy with earth-brown complexion, kind eyes, and a blue police cap, follows Edwin into the rear room. He is holding a notepad with Poppy's name and other things scrawled on the pages. The tallest of the two bobbies, a guy with earth-brown complexion, kind eyes, and a blue police cap, follows Edwin into the rear room.

The tallest of the two bobbies, a guy with earth-brown complexion, kind eyes, and a blue police cap, follows Edwin into the rear room. The most significant information in this passage is that Hazel has sent a package back to her previous employer and that it was her father, Edwin. The package and its contents now belong to Hazel, but she must pay for them, Edwin then informs her. But it won't come from Barnaby or her mother, Hazel swears to find a method to pay for them.

CHAPTER FOUR

Edwin presents Hazel with a handwritten invoice from Henry-Todd Publishing in New York that has Linda Andrews' contact information along with her address and phone number in Cape Cod, Massachusetts.

Hazel comes to the realization that the outrageous cost of the box is well worth the irreplaceable phone number of a location in Massachusetts where a woman by the name of Peggy Andrews wrote about Whisperwood. She then understands that Legrain, where writers and screenwriters worked in notebooks and sipped cappuccinos, is where she was supposed to meet Barnaby for dinner. Hazel enjoys sitting in Soho coffee cafes and overhearing conversations while drinking coffee. She takes the majority of the fall after slipping on the envelopes and landing forcefully on the wooden floors. She discovers a letter from Dorothy Bellamy requesting that she consider her perspective on the River Child.

The letter is torn in half and thrown in the trash by the woman. She then starts to clean up around the house by organizing the mail, folding clothes, making the bed, sweeping, and taking out the garbage. She raises the phone's green receiver to finish.

The Whisperwood novel and its original pictures are of interest to Hazel Linden, a bookseller at a rare book store in Bloomsbury. Since this is Hazel's first lead in twenty years, she needs to find out how she found out about the tale.

Hazel wants to know how the woman first learned of Whisperwood because the woman's voice is American and clipped. At nine in the morning, Peggy Andrews is startled to get a call from a woman named Hazel Linden. The woman informs her that her sister perished in the conflict and that the Whisperwood legend once had the power to save or destroy a young girl's life. When Peggy finds out that a woman in London read Whisperwood and claimed it as her own, she is astounded. When Peggy finds out that a woman in London read Whisperwood and claimed it as her own, she is astounded. When Peggy finds out that a woman in London read Whisperwood and claimed it as her own, she is astounded.

Hazel and Kelty are talking about Flora's disappearance, a six-year-old London child who vanished during the Blitz. Harry's sketches, some little larger than the palm of a child's hand, and other pieces of paper torn off textbook backs have been preserved by Hazel. Harry was accused of being obsessed with both of them and of torturing Flora by the police after they viewed his sketches of them. Others are drawn to Hazel and Kelty because of their vivid intensity. The most significant information in this passage is that Kelty and Hazel have been together for twenty years and that they have built Whisperwood, a mystical location, for Flora and themselves.

Although Kelty and Hazel have never returned to Binsey, Kelty is determined to find the book's author, Peggy Andrews, in order to protect the region from evil powers. Since Bridie and Harry haven't been in contact with Kelty and Hazel since they left, Kelty is determined to learn whether Bridie has ever heard of Whisperwood or has ever informed anybody else about it. Hazel is enraged at Kelty for leaving a family who had loved her and claims that it would have hurt too much for anyone to bring it all back.

Before their first meal together in Binsey, Hazel and Flora alternate trips to the restroom. They don matching corn-ower blue gowns and pull out a set of socks that Mum has carefully folded. Flora's hair is plaited by Hazel, who urges her to show courage. After dining out with Mrs. Aberdeen and her son, they wait for their mother to pick them up.

Four milk-colored glasses, four cream-colored china plates, green linen napkins, and Arthur Price silverware are used to arrange the meal.

The girls ate in silence as the staticky wifi droned on with the evening news. Harry finished the last fork and sat down. In the oven, Mrs. Aberdeen opened a tray of pudding cookies. Mrs. Aberdeen blessed the food once they had seated themselves and closed her hands in prayer. With his eyes closed, Harry grinned at her.

Mrs. Aberdeen straightened her posture and turned to face the girls. Harry's father had left by the time Flora enquired where he was. Hazel sat in silence, wondering if the word "gone" concealed a tale she should know. Mrs. Aberdeen gave a nod. Tomorrow, Mrs. Aberdeen, the mother of Hazel Linden, in Oxford, has extended an invitation to Flora and Mrs. Aberdeen.

When the day of the equinox comes, a goddess by the name of Persephone is compelled to enter the underworld once more. Flora answers Hazel's inquiry about why Persephone can't go by saying that she can leave for six months of the year and return to her mother on the vernal equinox. Flora says the stew is formal and sweet as Harry spins it on his spoon.

Sisters Bridie Mersey Linden and Hazel Mersey Linden reside in Binsey, England. Flora whispers to Hazel on their first night together in bed that she is nice and that they need to be patient.

Flora leads the group to Whisperwood, a mysterious location where anything can happen and where a river of stars winds through the forest. When Hazel discovers a glistening entrance, she follows Flora down the winding path to the river. Flora informs Hazel that she is coming and has a paw. The two most crucial facts in this passage are that Hazel and Flora are lionesses on their way to the river to drink stars and that they are staying with the Aberdeen family in a home in Binsey. In her dreams, Hazel sees a postcard flying over London before it crashes to the ground before getting there.

When she awakens to the sound of rain tinkling against the windowpanes and pattering on the roof, she finds a piece of paper hidden beneath the door. She examines Berry's pencil artwork as the morning's mellow light fills the room. The most significant information in this passage is that Flora is still asleep and that Bridie is preparing breakfast of porridge and sausage. In the kitchen, Hazel is hesitant to speak up for herself, but Bridie urges her to take a seat. The oatmeal has a lake of cream on top and is thick and lumpy.

CHAPTER FIVE

Bridie also says that she wishes she had a cow that produced sugar and that Harry will milk their cow at early light. Finally, Bridie assures Hazel that she will live in the Aberdeen home just like her and that Harry made the correct choice in picking her. Harry shows up jogging down the hill toward the home wearing a brown coat and a red knit cap. The sun also breaks through a low cloud as he does. The expanse of greenery and the ripple of the sky catch Hazel off guard.

Hazel runs to her sister's bedroom when she notices Flora in distress. Hazel is assured by Flora that she will never abandon her. Hazel travels to Oxford by rail on the Piccadilly line, where a cab driver lets her off at Port Meadow. She enters Binsey gently, taking it all in. A purple thistle and a jackrabbit with one ear shorter than the other are the only things Hazel touches when she pauses at the edge of Bridie's cottage's driveway.Then she passes The Perch, a bar, where Mr. Nolan waves and smiles amiably from the front stoop. They have gone about their daily ritual of The Times, two soft boiled eggs, tea, and toast, and he doesn't recognize Hazel.

Then, Hazel informs Barnaby that she is the owner of the Whisperwood pictures and that she will make amends with Edwin. Barnaby bids her farewell with a kiss before removing his coat from the hook near the front door. A young lady named Hazel has been residing in a cottage for a year.She is calmed by her mother, Bridie, who calls her name in a soothing tone. She is here for a reason, Bridie informs her, and she has been waiting for her to arrive. Hazel is reassured by her mother's care, and the inside of the cottage envelops her like a hug from Bridie. When Hazel and Bridie walk into the kitchen, Hazel sees a pair of enormous, muddy boots standing to the right of the rear door and a man's tweed jacket draped over a kitchen chair.

Bridie nods timidly and grins at Johnny Nolan, the town's religious pariah who weds the owner of the bar.Bridie responds by saying she is sorry for what occurred when Hazel questions why she has returned to her. Hazel and Bridie are talking about Flora, a little Bloomsbury girl who vanished. Hazel informs Bridie that she cooked up a tale about the land for Flora after Bridie accuses the police of being responsible for Flora's abduction. Hazel informs Bridie that Flora went looking for the land without her during their conversation over tea.

Hazel and Bridie both think Flora searched for the land without them, and so does Flora, according to Bridie.

Bridie thinks Hazel searched for a place named Whisperwood, which they use as a setting for their own tales. Bridie thinks Flora may have given the author her version of events and that everyone in the community was a suspect. Hazel is informed by Bridie that everyone in the community is a suspect and that the detectives are only doing their jobs. Bridie needs to let go of such thoughts, according to Hazel, who thinks that the earth snatched Flora from her. Due to Bridie's missing husband Harry and her later-lost child, the Aberdeen family had come under suspicion.

Bridie never heard from Harry again, and she was unaware that he had a wife and child of his own in Scotland. Harry was criticized by Bridie for his sketches, and she questioned him about them. Guilt and shame overcame Hazel, but Bridie informed her of St. Ives, a community of artists on the Cornish coast, which she had learned about from an art exhibit in Chelsea the previous month. Hazel is hesitant to face Harry while Bridie and she talk about his paintings. On St. Brigid's Day, they sat around a bonfire, but now she must battle her own dragons.

Although not much has changed in the cottage since Hazel left, she is back in the kitchen and seems to nearly recognize the girl she once was. Bridie tells Hazel the tale of Whisperwood.

At the Thames Valley Police Department, Chief Inspector Aiden Davies is waiting for the proper words to emerge under his palm when Hazel and Bridie arrive. He is unable to find the four nurses who resided behind the church, and Hazel tells him a folk tale about Flora going missing in Wallingford's bogs. Davies declines to provide Hazel with their names and contact information. Hazel is grieved by the loss of Flora, who she has known for twenty years, and he scratched his head once more while staring past her and muttering, "It ain't gonna do you no good." A sheet of paper containing the names of four ladies who are attempting to compose a story about Flora is offered to her by Aiden.

Hazel declines to provide the names to Dorothy Bellamy, who refers to Flora as "The River Child," on the grounds that they are private and she is unable to divulge any information. Aiden assures Hazel that this is theirs and that he won't reveal anything about Flora to her. Hazel had promised Barnaby she would meet him for dinner at Simpson's in the Strand when she got back to London from Oxford.

Despite being worn out and unprepared for the restaurant, she is adamant about getting there. She walks past the vibrantly colored storefronts of Liberty London and Carnaby Street, where jazz clubs were jam-packed with live music.

When she is on her way to see Barnaby, she criticizes herself for fretting about what she would wear to see Harry if she traveled to St. Ives. As tinny carnival music plays, an artist who is as slender as a twig presents his creations. Mid-step, Hazel stumbles and falls, but the artist picks her up. She fixes her gaze on his painting, an imitation of the well-known Max eld Parrish. Tenny and his friends are sharing a bottle of wine and smoking.

Without exchanging a single word, Tenny and Hazel have a moment of friendship just grinning at one other. The child held up his hands in submission as Tenny shoved him. Before entering the restaurant, Hazel waved over her shoulder. At a table next to the paneled wall, Barnaby was reading the menu. He grinned at Hazel and enquired as to her well-being.

He placed an order for a bottle of wine and calamari as an appetizer. She was questioned if she spent the entire day at Binsey. Barnaby drank his whisky slowly.

Although Hazel and Barnaby are set to embark on a new life, their history continues to follow them. Hazel is pulled close to Barnaby on her bed as he kisses her earlobe and offers to pay for the book's artwork.Barnaby urges her to take care of some things on her own, but she refuses. He draws her more closer, as if to refute her assertions.

That evening, Peggy and her mother Linda ate a simple meal. A weird phone conversation diverted Peggy, who then thought about her own life story for two days. She was more aware of the motivations of the characters in her books than she was of her own. She was questioned by Wren about her fear of the response. Peggy continued to face away from the story while claiming that when she was a young child, her mother and aunt Maria made it up as a means of providing Peggy with a secure getaway.

Garrett Witherspoon Andrews, Peggy's father, died during the attack on Pearl Harbor, and his body was returned to his family in a casket with an American flag draped over it. Linda, Peggy's mother, explained to her that the term Whisperwood was derived from the stories and that it combined elements of their respective stories—partly mine, partly hers, or perhaps Maria's.

Peggy lay awake in bed after they finished reading the pages from the previous day, just like the lightning outside. Although her memories of California were hazy and ragged, she wasn't scared. The origin stories of Peggy's world, Whisperwood, and Alastair Tennyson, Hazel Linden's son, are the most significant aspects in this novel.

After Daddy passed away, someone had given Peggy a short story to soothe her. When lightning struck a tree, Peggy leapt out of bed and discovered a crumpled piece of paper on which was written Hazel Linden's phone number. She tucked the piece of paper under her mattress and recalled the story of the princess and the pea, in which the tiny, insignificant pea served as a sensitivity test to see whether the princess was deserving of the prince. Hazel got out of the cab and stood at the end of a bluestone pathway after saying, "Yes, aren't we all tired enough of war?" to the driver. To avoid being exiled and the fear of being exiled, Hazel and Tennyson were transferred to the nation. Hazel's mother announced to her that she would wed Tennyson the following month, but she thought it was a betrayal.

Her father was 45 years old, and Flora had been gone for eleven years.

Flora's return to their family home required Mum to be present, so Hazel needed to believe that Flora was genuinely alive, was eleven years old, and needed Mum to be there. On her left ring finger, Hazel's mother, Mum, is wearing a sizable sapphire engagement ring. Hazel is outraged and wants to remain with her family, but her mother advises her to view it as a gift from her father. Then, Hazel admits her love for Tennyson, whom she had kissed in the hollow tree while momentarily losing sight of her sister.

Mum concurs, but Hazel is still troubled by Tennyson's ghostly presence on her front porch. Now is the moment to get rid of it. In order to celebrate Hazel's birthday, Tennyson and Hazel travel to the residence of Mrs. Alastair Tennyson. Hazel is welcomed by Mrs. Alastair Tennyson with a grin and is encouraged to pay her mother a visit. During the afternoon, Hazel and her mother, Mrs. Alastair Tennyson, decide to go shopping at Rodex.

Mrs. Alastair Tennyson, Hazel's mother, explains to her that happiness isn't always a result of marriage and having a child. Mrs. Alastair Tennyson, Hazel's mother, explains to her that happiness isn't always a result of marriage and having a child. Mum, Hazel's mother, is left in Bloomsbury alone to deal with whatever may occur.

She leaves to get breakfast and comes back to find Hazel sobbing. Hazel recalls spending her early years in a rowboat on Victoria Park's lake with Flora and Papa, as well as the day they traveled from London to the countryside.

Hazel explains that because her mother was working and they wouldn't billet an adult at the time, she was unable to travel to Binsey with her at the time. Hazel regrets her behavior but doesn't place the blame on her mother. The most significant information in this paragraph is that someone else knew about Whisperwood before Hazel told Flora and that Hazel and Flora used to make up stories about a river, a castle, and a location named Whisperwood. Hazel expresses regret to her mother for not informing Bridie of this prior to telling her. She also underlines that even if they miss Flora, they can still love each other.

Hazel ends by telling her mother that she loves both of them more than Flora and that they shouldn't let that stop them from loving. Mum, Hazel's mother, is making an effort to assist her daughter in getting over her love for someone or something. She hopes Flora, the book's author, told the narrative to it.

Alastair dashes into the room with a new moniker for Hazel that is less lyrical and shorter than her true name. At the gathering, Hazel is greeted by a towering man named Alastair.

He gives her a quick glance and a book of coagulated, uneaten eggs. Alastair leaves Hazel's narrative in Lorraine's capable hands and heads off to run his errands. Alastair kisses her, nods, and informs her that their kid is fourteen years old. Hazel grinned and gave him another kiss.

On their first day in Binsey, Bridie pushed Harry, Hazel, and Flora out of the house. She placed a rosemary stem in each of their coat pockets as protection. Flora fell to the ground outside after tripping over an enamel milking can. Flora took Harry's hand as he extended it to her and stood up. Harry grinned and wished them welcome to the nation.

The river, which serves as Harry and Flora's guide to the land's edge, welcomes them. Harry leads them down a well-traveled dirt route, past homes with thatched roofs on calm streets and past horn bush hedges that are fading and have leaves falling from the trees. As a punting boat with three ladies rowing it passed them while laughing and attempting to stay upright, they arrived at the river's side and stood next to Harry.

Black and white cows graze across the river, nosing into the grasses and eating idly. In the river, Harry and Hazel discover what they think to be their own upside-down universe.Harry leads them through a protracted route till they reach a stone chapel, where Flora is gathering leaves in her robe. Harry then takes them to the towns of Padstow and Wolvercote, where a boat house is located and the river separates around a small island. They then proceed to Oxford and Jericho by way of the meadow. At St. Margaret's Church, where they are walking on the dead, Harry and Flora arrive. They will have to return later to find the door that Flora noticed hidden behind a twee.

Harry's way in the world makes Hazel feel fear, and she spots a gray, shingled home behind the parish church with smoke curling from its chimney and a table on its front porch. The rector's home is generally the rector's home, although nurses from the hospital dwell there while he stays in a guest room at the Baldwins' house. Hazel and Flora follow Harry to a rectangular stone wall encircling an aperture in the dirt, where they find a wellhead of water buried in shadow. Harry explains that treacle is molasses, sweets and sugar, and the Dormouse narrates the story of three daughters living at the bottom of a treacle well. The narrative of Saint Margaret's Well is told by Harry and Flora.

CHAPTER SIX

It is about an Oxford princess named Frideswide who ran away from the King of Mercia, Algar, to become his bride. When Algar was near to marrying her, he was struck by lightning and blinded, so he would never be able to locate her again. This story is a reminder of the necessity of going after someone you love, even if it means running away.

Hazel Linden, a twenty-one year old student at Newnham Hall of Cambridge, receives a letter from Harry Aberdeen asking her to explain her record of flawless performance at Hogan's. Kelty, a friend of Hazel's, pushes her to focus on what's ahead today, and Hazel agrees to meet him.

Hazel had been waiting for her to see him since Binsey, and the war was done, but rationing of commodities like sugar and chocolate lingered. Her papa was gone and Flora remained a mystery that even Oxford's detectives couldn't solve. Hazel had been expecting a letter from Harry Aberdeen, the lad she had pinned to the ground at school and helped them look for Flora.

She had been waiting for the letter for several years, but it never arrived. One night at a lecture by J.R.R.Tolkien, she got a letter from Scotland from Ethan Baldwin, the kid she'd pinned to the ground at school and helped them hunt for Flora. She read the letter slowly, changing her mind from how she'd envisioned Harry's last six years to the man he might be today. Bridie had wished to protect Harry Aberdeen from rumor and scandal. He had graduated and attended University of Edinburgh, studying mathematics.

Hazel had pledged to never see him again, but a letter was not the same as meeting him. They wrote for three years, telling each other of their lives. Hazel graduated in 1948 and obtained a job at The Crown, drawing Guinness and pouring whiskey. Over the course of that year, she informed Harry about all of it, such as the odor of chemicals rising through the floorboards, the books she read, and the lips that moved while she read. Hazel Linden's vow to be the person Harry knew in letters remained intact, but she made a new promise to be the person who Harry knew in letters.She heeded her mum's advice and applied for a job at Hogan's. Three hours into the drive, Hazel stopped into a station for more petrol and Kelty joined her for a picnic in the gardens of Rougemont Castle.

Hazel missed her child, Midge, and the beautiful countryside in the spring. Hazel and Kelty visit Rougemont Castle in Northernhay Gardens, where they find a picnic table and wooden bench. Hazel informs Kelty that the castle is constructed of white and gray stone and that Flora felt she had dreamt Bridie's residence into being.

Kelty explains that the Devon witches were tried here in 1680, the last to be hanged for being witches in England. Hazel wonders what Harry looks like now, but Kelty doesn't care. Hazel and Kelty are driving to St. Ives, Cornwall, to meet Harry. They arrive at the Sloop Inn, founded in 1312, and are greeted by couples and singles enjoying wine and gaze out to sea. They check in, unpack, have a pint, and then meet Harry at the Sloop Inn.

When they leave, Kelty asks if she loves him and Hazel shakes her head. Hazel and Kelty meet at a café table in St. Ives, England. Kelty tells Hazel she looks lovely in a cerulean shift dress with pockets and a Peter Pan collar. They debate the artist colony in St. Ives, which is both adored and reviled for its Bohemians, true artists, and stinky vagabonds. Hazel and Kelty decide to tour the artist colony together.

Harry is standing in front of an easel beside a high iron-mullioned window with his left hand in midair, holding a paintbrush, and his right hand tapping a rhythm on lion-colored slacks. Hazel and Kelty are standing at the open door, and three other artists are at work. Bobby Darin is performing "Dream Lover" while the rear door is open. Kelty jumps out screaming "Harry!" Harry recognizes her and holds her in his arms, one on each side, pulling them close. Hazel marvels how he has become a man, this guy.

Time swooped back in as Harry stood back, yet kept one hand on each of their shoulders. Hazel and Kelty meet Harry and Ethan Baldwin, two childhood friends from Binsey, in the Sloop Inn tavern. Hazel informs Harry that she saw her mother and Mr. Nolan, and that they were blind. Harry proposes they settle in and reminisce in the bar, but Hazel wants them to ask a single question. The four sit together at a table for two, with Ethan on her other side.Awkwardness replaces the early euphoria at the studio, and Kelty recommends an artist colony. Harry and Hazel are discussing their lives and occupations. Harry is a painter who has been living in Cornwall for ten years and is waiting for his big break.

He is married to Fergus and has a daughter named Midge. Ethan is married to a crazy man, Fergus, and is trying to bust out in the art world.Hazel is married to a professor, Barnaby, who is a professor. Harry and Hazel are discussing their lives and occupations. Hazel and Kelty are astonished to learn that Ethan's brother Adam has migrated to America 10 years ago and is now the garment king of Manhattan's Lower East Side. Hazel asks Harry if he may stroll down to the river with her for a minute, and he agrees. They proceed down concrete stairs and reach a wet strip of beach, where a brilliant blue rowboat lays on its side with a red buoy swinging from a barnacle-covered rope.

They proceed down concrete stairs and reach a wet strip of beach, where a brilliant blue rowboat lays on its side with a red buoy swinging from a barnacle-covered rope. Harry perched on the side of a boat and smiled to see Hazel. She adjusted her foot in the sand, felt it give way beneath her. He interrupted her thoughts and chastised her for losing her sister Flora. She felt as if she was betraying her sister, breaking a vow.He interrupted her thoughts and chastised her for losing her. She wanted to see him again and know he was well. He asked her about the name of their land, which she told Flora about.

CHAPTER SEVEN

Harry and Hazel recount a story about their argument by the side of the river. Hazel tells Harry the entire narrative, from the day she found the book Whisperwood to this moment on the beach.

He listens without moving, scarcely blinking, and pulls her against his chest without a word. She asks Harry if Flora disappeared hunting for Whisperwood, but he shook his head and left her alone. She understands that they could have been bearing the same burden of guilt all these time.

St. Brigid's Day and Imbolc were celebrated at the beginning of February, with a bon re, colored wool blankets, an old farm table, cheeses, fruits, fresh baked bread, and a large jug of red wine. Four nurses, Frances, Maeve, Imogene, and Lilly, played with Flora more than they talked to the townspeople, as though their mission was to guard the tiniest of them. Father Fenelly and Mr. Nolan laughed about something Mr. Nolan said. The twins, Ethan and Adam, kicked about a leather ball with Harry and another child from town, who had asked if they were orphans. Hazel and Flora had been living with the Aberdeens for four months, and Bridie marked the seasons with rituals and candles and scented sticks.

Kelty had made it safely to Piccadilly by train with money she'd taken from the hag's kitchen counter. Hazel wrote back to Kelty, telling her about Binsey, Mr. Nolan and his dog, Mackey, the town event for Christmas Eve, and the Baldwin twins. Bridie had her own style of speaking, and she never spoke Hitler's name. Hazel and Flora have been visiting their mother, Mum, for the holidays and every few weeks, but have never taken her to Whisperwood. One winter day, Mum came to spend the whole day and even the night with them, and they tried to cheer her up by playing jacks, demonstrating her newfound knowledge, and combing through academic sheets.

After a warm dinner, it was time for Mum to tuck them in. Hazel went out silently to sit in the corridor between the kitchen and living room, listening to the rise and fall of Mum and Bridie's chat. Hazel and her mother, Bridie, are commemorating St. Brigid's Day with a party to appreciate the seasons, each other, and remember that they are part of something bigger than the trivial concerns of today. Bridie says that St. Brigid is the saint of Imbolc, the advent of creativity, spring, and fresh growth, and that she invites us to ask what we want to bring forth into this world in the following year.

Hazel and her mother, Mr. Nolan, are also honoring St. Brigid's Day with a party to appreciate the seasons, each other, and remember that they are part of something bigger than conflict.

Hazel and Maeve are nurses at St. Hugh's Hospital. Imogene is crying and Maeve is holding her arm around her. Imogene tells Hazel that a soldier was gone and she couldn't save him. Hazel hurries to Bridie and Flora, warming herself by the stove and swearing to never tell Flora what she'd heard. Later, Imogene grabs Flora by the hand, dancing around and around until they collapse on the chilly ground.

Frances murmurs that this is not a pagan ritual and that it is Saint Brigid, a goddess. Hazel, Frances, Imogene, and Father Finally gather for last goodbyes as Bridie thanked all who had come and lifted her voice to everyone. Father Fenelly encourages them to trust their love, serve their purpose, and worship their name, through Jesus Christ our Lord. Flora falls asleep in Imogene's arms and Harry jostles her awake. Flora asks Harry if magic is real, and he offers out his hand to take her inside.

Bridie is a pagan who believes in nature and uses old legends to make new ones. She urges Hazel to construct her own pagan myths and to select what is good and real, not what would ruin. She and Hazel go inside to make sure Harry has tucked Flora into bed and that Harry isn't completing the lion puzzle again. Hazel and Bridie walk back to the house and Hazel enters with warmth.

The St. Ives tavern is filled with Irish jigs and a short woman performing Irish jigs on the ddle. Kelty watches from the round table, as Hazel seems dizzy from dancing with Harry. They reach the shore and stand at the edge at high tide, when the lighthouse glow reveals his face. Hazel realizes that if she lets Harry touch her, it would destroy her and drown Flora again. Kelty invites her to stay with him for a bit, and she wakes up in the next bed.

Hazel and Harry had a lovely time together on the beach last night, exchanging stories of their lives over the past twenty years. Hazel and Kelty had planned to visit Whisperwood, but Kelty decided to go home instead. Hazel had thought about Barnaby, but only with guilt because if he had seen them, he would have been upset and enraged. Kelty was pleased to be both carsick and hungover.

Kelty and Hazel are driving home from St. Ives when Kelty stops to marvel at the water and the fishermen pushing to sea with their nets.

He then informs Hazel that Harry Aberdeen was a suspect and that his mother had made him disappear. Barnaby arrives at Hazel's home and tells her that Harry was never accused of foul play. Hazel contends that things weren't the way they looked and that Barnaby had arrived late that night after she'd returned from St. Ives. Barnaby is angry at Hazel for not having seen Harry since he left Binsey twenty years ago. Hazel spots the letters she had left in the trunk in the hall closet.

Barnaby adds that the letters are melancholic letters of two people in love, and Hazel still loves him. He asks her whether she still loves him and she says that she still loves him. Barnaby and Hazel are discussing their childhood and the loss of Flora. Barnaby is hunting for a fairy tale in a book published by an American author, and Hazel is worried about her preoccupation with the book. Barnaby apologizes for her fixation and begs her to calm down. They both lost someone, and Hazel's story could be affected by the book.

Peggy Andrews runs to Wren's house with a telegram that she believes is life and death. Wren brings her to the shore and she offers him a thin paper to read. He informs her that Oscar Wilde once remarked that telling "beautiful untrue things" was the objective of art. She informs him that she is reporting back from an invisible place, where words and curses and spells have power and there is magic. He nods and kisses her cheek, saying she is special and her stories usually have happy ends.

The most crucial aspects in this book are that Peggy and Wren are running across an ancient fairy-tale figure in Grimm's original fairy tales, and that they are traveling to London to find the woman and assist her resolve her own story. Wren has a passport, and Peggy has a passport from a trip to Canada her senior year. Mother is stalking them, with her black coat spreading behind her like the wings of a big crow. Peggy and Wren are so close that if he chooses, they can kiss. Wren and Peggy meet at midnight to begin on a mission to find Whisperwood, a magical telegram from a witch who returns to take the princess back to her tower.

Peggy is unhappy at her mother for shielding her, but Mother assures her that Whisperwood is theirs and they have made it truly their own. Wren and Peggy go to the beach at midnight with luggage, and Peggy finds Whisperwood in her pocket.

Mother says that Whisperwood is a magical telegram from a witch who returns to take the princess back to her tower. Peggy's mother pulls out a crumpled phone number from her dress and asks her why she is asking about the land's name and who called it Whisperwood. Mother cautions her of crazy people who will try to take what's hers.

Peggy plans to meet Wren around midnight, but her mother refuses to answer her questions. Peggy is tired of thinking and wondering and wants to have her own experience with Wren. She retrieves her small round bag from beneath her bed and folds silk matching sets of underwear, two owered dresses, a pair of dark blue trousers, and a cashmere blue cardigan. She tiptoes down the hallway and out the back door, feeling as if she had left her own home.

Hazel and Barnaby are visiting an art display in Hampstead with Kelty, Fergus, Midge, and Harry Aberdeen. Barnaby asks Hazel if she loves the man she stood on the sidewalk with, but she denies it. He then informs her that his father assisted her get the position at Sotheby's and they phoned him about Hogan's and the illustrations. Hazel says that her father helped her acquire the position and that he made a few calls about the stolen book and pictures. He then tells her that he is betraying all of them.

The most significant information in this text are that Hazel and Barnaby are not lovers and that they are departing for Paris in two days. Hazel then reads an article in Vanity Fair magazine about a little girl from Hillingdon, Beryl Myatt, who died when the ship she was on was bombed on September 17, 1940. She cannot allow Flora to be one more of Dorothy Bellamy's melodramatic stories, as she cannot allow Flora to be one more of her melodramatic stories. The most crucial elements in this essay are the four nurses from Binsey who were interviewed and exonerated of suspicion of foul play relating to Flora in September of 1940. Hazel was astonished to see a letter from Barnaby carrying a note in Aiden's block handwriting regarding the four nurses and their addresses and phone numbers.

Barnaby then kissed Hazel and stashed the Whisperwood stories in school notebooks. After the Imbolc, Hazel started writing down the Whisperwood stories in school notebooks and buried them in the bottom dresser drawer. Hazel and Flora experienced a snowfall in late February, trapping them in the house with a roaring stove, schoolwork, and stacks of books. Hazel wrote about the day's activities, adding magical components, as if Whisperwood had ceased to be fictional.

On the twentieth of May, Flora and Hazel raced to the meadow and found it changed into a chaotic area of bell-shaped tents and troops. Bridie stated that it was an operation to help the British Expeditionary Force and allied troops who had been rescued from Dunkirk. The morning after breakfast, Harry, Flora, and Hazel hurried out the door and saw the men and encampment. Harry was proud of Britain and pledged to join them when he could, but Hazel refused, thinking of her papa and the day of his departing. Flora and Hazel are on a meadow near a river.

Flora is anxious about her sister's safety, but Hazel pushes her to go where she might be killed. Flora pulls at the edges of Hazel's flowered dress and asks whether Papa is over there. Hazel chases her sister and discovers Harry seated near them on the wet grass. Flora buries her face in Harry's neck and wonders if he can bring Papa back. Harry and Hazel lock eyes over Flora's downy hair and Harry plucks a ragwort ower from the ground.Hazel kisses Harry on the cheek and Flora lowers her head to reveal a crescent of blood on her middle finger. The four nurses gather at the river's side and Frances accuses Harry of smuggling a little sugar over an innocent girl's head. Imogene, the one with the raven-dark hair who often babysat, tells Flora that her papa is not over there.

Imogene, Hazel, and Flora had a lovely life in Whisperwood, England, as war raged on. Bridie crocheted thick socks for the soldiers, cooked pickled cucumbers and onions, taught them to make rabbit and lamb pies, and hiked the woods with Bridie.

They learned the difference between stonewort, violet, meadow mushrooms, hogweed, and nightingale. They also swam in the river, watched Harry with the other Binsey boys play cricket, and sat on the grass and watched Harry with the other Binsey boys play cricket. On the July day of Flora's sixth birthday, Hazel and Flora were in the woodlands, dashing between thicketed oaks and alders until they found the shimmering door of Whisperwood. They slid into the hollow and chanted their spell to reach the palace that waits. Flora was losing her lisp and Hazel was heartbroken, losing her babyhood.

The starry river runs quickly and the sun is dazzling, and the wild stags on the far side are looking at them. Flora and Hazel arrive at the castle, where the queen greets them with glee. Flora asks if everyone is worthy, and Hazel laughs at her. They return to the genuine woodlands of Binsey, where Harry stands at the edge of the wild ower eld with gooseberries green and veined hanging over a stone wall next to him.

CHAPTER EIGHT

Hazel brings Flora to Harry, who is wearing his summer khaki-colored pants and a white linen short-sleeved shirt that Bridie had stitched new buttons on only last night.

Flora breaks into a full run, but Hazel pulls back. Hazel uses the queen's voice as her own when she returns to the cottage. She sees her mother crying in her pink dress, recalling the day when she had walked into the rear garden of Mecklenburgh Square and held out the note of evacuation. She tells her that the McWhorter's son was killed in a battle in Belgium three nights ago. Bridie and Flora appear at the doorway and Hazel is lifted and held by them.

Hazel rushed away from Flora to hide the McWhorters from her sister, Flora. The next night, the stars were strong enough to light the meadow and Hazel snuggled down on the plaid blanket with Flora. Harry plopped down next to her, staring at the sky in silence until he questioned, "What are you doing?" Hazel cried softly and took his hand, wounding it through hers. He asked her how the stars make her feel better, but not tonight.

Harry and Hazel are talking about the stars and how they make them feel better. He explains that there are people smarter than him who are trying to figure out where the stars come from. He kisses her tenderly and lingers long enough for her to feel better. He sweeps his hand through her hair and she asks if he took some of the grief from her.

Hazel's impetuous choice to ride the train to Henley-on-Thames was as impulsive as taking the book from Hogan's. She had contacted all three nurses, but Imogene Wright never answered the phone. She took her coat from the hanger and was on her way to Piccadilly train station. When she got to the park, a man on an iron bench offered her a croissant and asked her where she was headed. She grinned and said she was traveling to Henley-on-Thames for a story.

Harry shrugged and stated it wasn't a good choice. Harry and Hazel are traveling to Henley-on-Thames to talk to a nurse who resided in Binsey. They encounter Iris Taber, a nurse with a name similar to Hazel's Flora. Hazel is scared that if a nurse abducted Flora and brought her out to raise her, Aiden would find out. Harry tells her that he had come to see her once, a year after her last letter, and that he should have told her when he first met her.

Harry and Hazel meet at a park seat in Henley-on-Thames, near London and Oxford. They discuss St. Ives and Harry's art. They go by white-plaster homes , a market and bakery. The Thames, thought to have snatched Flora from them, flows fast towards London. Harry kisses Hazel's palm in such a delicate gesture that she wants to wrap her arms around him until the picture of Flora's body at the bottom of the river goes forever.

Harry and Hazel are looking for 17 Allington Way, the home of Iris Muldoon and her mother, Imogene. They locate the house with a dark wood front door with an iron Celtic cross knocker, two windows on either side of the front entrance with window boxes beneath them, and a low white fence with an iron scrolled gate. Ivy crawls up the west wall of the home, working its way around the corner to the front. Harry draws her close and kisses her cheek. The midday sun sends their shadows across the cobbled lane.

Iris Taber is a small woman with blond hair and brown eyes. She is a nurse in the village during the war with Operation Pied Piper and lives with the Aberdeen family. Iris smiles at

Harry and asks him an odd question: How old are you? Hazel rips apart the woman's face in small bits and pieces and realizes that she is not Flora, twenty years later. Harry's grin, soft voice, and friendly atmosphere encourage the woman to relax again.

Harry and Iris visit Hazel's mother's house in Bloomsbury to discuss Flora, Hazel's sister, who disappeared when her mother lived in Binsey. Harry's sketch of Flora sprinting towards something hazy in the foreground is one of her faves. Hazel wakes up with a foggy dream of Father Fenelly laughing and talking to her mother. She drops Harry's drawing on the dresser for Flora to see when she awoke. In the kitchen, Bridie is gone and the beat-up Flying Nine is gone.

Frost kisses the window's edges, beginning to melt with the rising sun. Hazel and Flora are in Binsey, England, waiting for the news of the bombing of London. They turn on the wireless and hear an announcement that London had been bombed. Bridie and Harry arrive and tell them that Kelty is in hospital and her mother is okay. Kelty's mother is killed and Bridie's voice breaks as tears pour from her eyes.

Hazel's heart floods with fear. The most crucial elements in this chapter are that Flora and Hazel's mother, Bridie, has sent Kelty to her aunt in Lancashire, and that Kelty is in hospital, hurt but alive. Hazel's father is lost in action and Flora's mother, Bridie, is unable to bring Kelty to the hag. Three days later, their mother comes to Binsey, telling them about London's horrors and their schooling. Hazel's mother, Flora, rides her bicycle to and from her job at the war office and runs to the air raid shelter in the Tube as the sirens whirl.

Hazel crawled next to Mum on the couch in the middle of the night, thinking of Kelty without a mum. In the morning, Mum went without waking her. Hazel packed her rucksack, rubber mask, and name badge, and hurried outdoors in the rain. She asked Bridie to take her with her. Hazel and their mother are cuddled under an umbrella and Flora and Harry are looking from the cottage's front door.

Hazel refuses to take her with them on the train, but she swears to come anyhow. Mum is taking no chances with her, and Hazel vows to return to Bridie this afternoon. She crawls inside Bridie's car.

Imogene Mulroney sat across from Hazel and Harry at her daughter Iris' kitchen table in Henley-on-Thames. She was a small woman with vivid blue eyes and muddy-colored locks. Hazel inquired if Imogene recalled Flora, a sprite who she prays for every October 19th and remembers on St. Frideswide's feast. Imogene glanced between Harry and Hazel and remembered them as two peas in a pod. Iris pulled a pan of shortbread from the oven as her child ran about the house looking for an imagined rabbit.

The police arrived to talk to all of them, but no one saw or knew anything. The most crucial information in this text are that Hazel, the police inspector, provided her the name and address of all the nurses, and that Frances, an American nurse from the Red Cross, came over expecting to meet a British boy and fall in love. She had romantic illusions and thought of herself as Florence Nightingale, who would wash the brows of the fallen boys. Imogene tried her hardest to save the lads, but couldn't save them. Hazel tried to grasp the truth with Imogene, and found a kernel of something that would take her to Flora.

Iris, Imogene, Harry, and Hazel are discussing Flora's death. Iris is enamored of Flora, while Imogene is enamored of her own kid.

Iris's father, Martin, is working in the marketplace and they have the sole market in town. Iris and Hazel are grieved by Flora's death, but Harry encourages them to let it go. Hazel slams her hand on her leg, stating she can't un-know things.

Hazel is battling to save her life, but Harry is attempting to convince her that breaking away isn't always simple. She pushes at him and he quips that it proves he cares.

In the early dark of evening, Harry stands at the doorway of Hazel's at and she doesn't unlock the door. He tries to welcome her in, but she refuses. She then unlocks the door, enters, and closes it without glancing back.

She stands alone in the Bloomsbury at, where she has witnessed loss before. Hazel and her mother travel to the Russell Square Station, where they pass a ragged British bag, a life-size dollhouse, a woman in tattered clothing with three little children, and an unharmed butcher store adjacent to a demolished café. The environment has altered enough to be both recognizable and not, with dust covering lampposts and cars, stores with blown-out windows, and black curtains billowing in the broken holes. Hazel's scribbled list of persons who might have heard about her enchanted place encourages her to believe that the extraordinary can imbue the ordinary one more time.

Hazel's mother tells her that the neighborhood was bombed two nights before and that the bombers use the Thames as a map into the city.

Hazel's mother informs her that they are crowded into underground platforms and that Hazel and Flora are keeping away so that one day they can come back. Hazel's mother reassures her that they are happy Bridie selected her girls and that they must keep safe. Hazel and her mother visit the Great Ormond Street Hospital, where Kelty is meant to be. The ward is full with white iron beds and cribs, and a boy sat as a nurse read to him. A little woman donned a lace nurse's cap and stooped over an infant dozing in a cot, patting its back.

White lamps dropped puddles of dazzling light on the bedside tables, while colorful ribbons dangled from several mattresses. Hazel sees Kelty on the far side of the room, with her eyes closed and a bandage covering her arm and forehead. She tells them she will come and they don't believe her. Kelty is sent to her aunt Bernice in Lancashire, and Hazel wishes to bring her some ribbons to bring back to Binsey. The nurse with the lace cap comes at the bedside of the kid next to Hazel, who has black letters painted on her forehead: M 14.

CHAPTER NINE

Matron Lane studies the chart at the end of the child's bed, then turns to Hazel and Mum. She tells them that Kelty has received a fourth dose of morphine and that they are relatives. Matron Lane asks Hazel if she is kin to Kelty, a youngster with lettering on her forehead. Hazel agrees, but Flora tells her that Kelty is all right and her aunt Bernice will take her home tomorrow. Hazel resolves not to tell Flora of the hospital or the bandages or ribbons or the child with writing on her forehead.

Flora then cries, moving away from Hazel and curling into herself. Hazel discovers that the death of Whisperwood wasn't her fault, but the bombs, war, and nasty man with a mustache had. The weather was unusually high for October, and Bridie warned Hazel it would be the final warm day in Binsey before winter rolled in. She had tidied the garden and the trees outside the cottage had shed their leaves. As the months passed, Harry and Hazel never spoke of the kiss and their night under the stars, but the longing for him consumed her in the oddest hours. Harry had drawn the letters in varied colors, each with an image underneath that started with the letter.

Flora was learning her letters, and Harry had drawn the letters in varied colors, each with an illustration underneath that started with the letter.

These words were glimpses of their secret place and yet Whisperwood was gone. On St. Frideswide's Day, Bridie packed a picnic basket with cheese and slabs of ham, performed a song about a tisket and tasket, and set a red wool blanket on top. She took her car into Oxford to pay for a new phone and have the lines brought over her sweeping eld for terrible news. When they approached the river's banks, Flora bumped into Hazel and nearly sent her into the surging water. Harry rushed behind them, carrying the picnic meal Bridie had packed, and the river surged strong as though late for its destiny.

Hazel nearly fell into the fast-moving water when Flora ran into her. Over the past few months, Hazel and Harry have spent time together and exchanged stories about their lives—both in and out of the woods. They share a bedroom, and Harry gives her good morning and good night kisses. Harry inquires as to whether Hazel has been snooping on them as she tells Flora one of their stories. He blushes as she assures him that she would never spy on them.

Hazel queries how he learned of their tales now that they are face to face. In the late afternoon of an autumn day, Harry and Hazel are relaxing in a tiny cottage. When Harry inquires about their location in secret, Hazel feels embarrassed but won't give him the one item that she and Flora share. She rushes to the hollow tree and cavernous area of Whisperwood and enters it while closing her eyes, feeling enraged, needy, scared, depressed, and yearning for Harry. When Harry eventually calls, she picks up.

In the Savoy Hotel in London, Wren and Peggy are intertwined in a canopy bed. Wren explains to Peggy that fairy tales are about beasts, Gulliver is about a traveler, and Alice in Wonderland is about dreams. Peggy explains that Aesop's tales are about beasts, Gulliver is about a traveler, and Alice in Wonderland is about dreams.

Peggy concurs with Wren's suggestion that these stories have been divided up. Fairy tales and other stories are the topic of a conversation between Wren and Peggy. Wren explains that he was expelled from Harvard as a result of cheating in a chemistry class.

A happy ending, a new perspective on the world, and some sort of recovery are all things that Peggy says a fairy tale is supposed to provide for us. Their bodies reunite as Wren wraps his leg around hers.

The last time that Aiden Davies, Hazel, Harry, and Bridie saw Flora is something they can all recall. Harry ran back to the house to tell Bridie about her departure, and Hazel ran up and down the riverbank yelling, "Flora Lea! With sirens screeching along Binsey Lane, the police arrived quickly and with a lot of noise. Bridie questioned Hazel about her whereabouts, her reason for being by herself, her time away, and her motivation for fleeing Harry. She wished she could go back to the instant when she had fled from Harry.

A teddy bear named Flora had fallen into the river without coming out, so Hazel and her friends race to the riverbanks to find her. They follow Aiden Davies' advice to look for footprints, but they don't come across any. Despite the cold and how quickly the river is moving, Hazel jumps in and finds only rocks. When Imogene watched Flora, she and Harry had waded into the shallows, but this time, the river was much colder and higher. Aiden Davies, a police officer who is bigger, stronger, and made of steel, saves Hazel.

They liberate Hazel from Mrs. Marchman's grasp; she was the witch who stole Flora to stand in for Kelty. Running past The Perch, the school, and Mrs. Marchman's home, Hazel flees at top speed. Together, they rescue Flora from Mrs. Marchman's grasp after hearing Harry running behind her. Mrs. Marchman must have been watching and waiting in the woods for the right moment to kidnap Flora. A tire on its side, a broken hoe with rusted teeth, and a defeated white fence attenuated over a lifeless garden can all be found in the yard in front of Mrs. Marchman's home. Flora is not being returned as Hazel screams for her, but Mrs. Marchman is unaware of the drama unfolding next to the nearby River Thames.

Heather swipes Harry's corduroys and Hazel's bare legs as Harry and Hazel run to the church, where the steeple of the church pierces the setting sun like a needle in a pink balloon. Hazel had a dream about Harry the night before she and Barnaby left for Paris. In her dream, Harry was surrounded by untamed owers at the edge of a river. He didn't hear her until she woke up, even though she was calling his name. Flora, who had never been left alone at night, was located at the well by Aiden Davies, Father Fenelly, Ethan Baldwin, and a small number of the town residents.

Hazel inquired about Flora's whereabouts in the river, but Aiden gave her a glare and told her it was pointless.

The policeman glared at Aiden and spat out the word "magical" with disdain. Aiden threw his coat over Hazel's shoulders as she was stumbling and queasy. Hazel is writing her story while having a nightmare. She is comforted by Barnaby, who also urges her to let it out. After kissing her neck, he advises her to get rid of Harry.

She pours herself a cup of tea and assures him that her parents are sympathetic. Harry is not the issue, according to Barnaby, but everything else is. In ten hours, Barnaby and Hazel will cross the English Channel on the Night Ferry. To get to Victoria, they will take the Charing Cross, then get on the sleeping car. When the train reaches Dover, it detaches from the rails and the entire vehicle pulls up alongside the ship.

Hazel is wearing a pillbox hat, black ballet flats, and her classiest travel outfit. Above the open latticework arching over the station, the evening sky has softened. The best items from Hazel's wardrobe, including silk dresses with matching hats and lingerie she'd purchased especially for the trip, are packed in her two suitcases. While traveling by train with Barnaby, Hazel is looking for a story's author.

Despite Hazel's desire to stick it out and find a lasting love, they decide to change their itinerary and head to Boston instead of Paris.

They encounter Kelty, a woman wearing an owl brooch, who instructs them to get off the train. Kelty orders Hazel to stop trying to make sense of the meaningless and the senseless. Hazel falls down the stair after Barnaby releases her hand. While saying their goodbyes, Kelty and Midge bring Hazel a box of chocolates to enjoy on the train. A note from Peggy Andrews, who is currently in London, requests to meet Hazel tomorrow at 9 a.m. in the lobby of The Savoy. Kelty is holding out the note. Reading the note, which instructs her to pick between herself and Peggy Andrews, Hazel grabs Barnaby's arm.

Hazel and Harry are in Binsey because Hazel's mother has sent them gifts and has come to see them. She finds herself lying in the back of a car with her head on Harry's lap when she awakens. She is left in the kitchen by herself, pinned down by blankets and a hot water bottle. The adults are organizing search teams and dispatching others to contact the nearby villages, but Hazel won't reveal the date of Frideswide's passing.

She finds her stories about Whisperwood and Harry's drawings when she opens the bottom dresser drawer.

In search of something that doesn't exist, Hazel drags her sister into a fast-moving river. In order to get to the riverbank where she had lost Flora, she unlocks the window and squeezes through it. Her slippers catch on the nettles that stung her feet as she lifts the pages and takes them off. She observes horrifying images of Flora falling into the water as she walks along the river without falling in. The pages yaw away as she opens her hand, falling to the bottom of the swiftly flowing river.

As she made her way through the night to St. Margaret's church, Hazel confronted Jesus and begged him to take Flora back. She rubbed the blood from her ankle on the marble altar and vowed never to make up a story or flee to Whisperwood again. She recited the vow three times as the church's cries rang against the wet stones and echoed. She returned to the cottage and climbed through the window to the vacant bed. She was shaken awake in the wee hours of the morning by her mother.

Hazel awakens in the hospital with a fever and an arm-tethered glass bottle of clear liquid. She recalls Aiden Davies standing next to Harry and Bridie on the front porch with a notebook and a sad expression, as well as her own vow to never see or speak to Harry again. After three days, Hazel gives in to the despair quicksand and vows to locate Flora. She is being sought after by Constable Davies, and Hazel promises to find her when she gets up. The fact that Hazel and her mother, Mum, were abandoned in Oxfordshire during the Blitz is one of the text's most significant details.

Hazel refused to accept that she had drowned, even though Constable Davies thought she had. Hazel and her mother stayed in Oxford for two months, spending days stumbling through the streets and wooded areas of Oxfordshire in search of her sister Flora. For eight months, the Blitz persisted, and throughout that time, Hazel and Mum each carried their own grief. Sometimes they handled it differently, and other times they found themselves on the same sea of sorrow. The most crucial information in this passage is that both Hazel and Mum feared losing Hazel to the same fate as Flora and her husband. Hazel looked for someone to blame but never looked in the mirror.

Hazel later traveled to Cambridge University to pursue her studies in literature after leaving London. She kept watching for a laughing young woman with blond curls in the imaginary woods. When the church bells rang on May 7, 1945, Hazel had graduated and was working at Hogan's in London.

In order to request access to the newspaper archives, Peggy Andrews and Wren Andrews fly to London and take a taxi to the British Library in North London. The articles about Flora Lea Linden, who had been cherished by her family, were read by them. Peggy wonders how her family could cope with this loss and is overcome by the sadness and mystery of it. While she waits for Mum and Kelty to arrive, Hazel Linden sips her tea while standing at her kitchen counter. Barnaby was supposed to wake up in a sleeper car with Hazel, but she abandoned him on the platform.

Midge was perplexed when Kelty helped her with the luggage. She made an attempt to apologize to Barnaby, but he cut her off. Wren kissed Peggy after they exchanged glances in the mirror. They walked down the lengthy green carpeted hallway after leaving the hotel room. When Hazel and Kelty arrive at The Savoy, they see a roundabout full of taxis coming and going from the hotel's red-lettered façade.

Hazel gives a trill of love in response to Kelty's question about whether she would recognize Flora if she saw her. As they enter the lobby, Kelty asks if they know what Peggy Andrews looks like, and Hazel makes fun of her best friend. Peggy pauses to admire the blooms and feels the edge of a yellow dahlia to confirm that everything is genuine. While awaiting Hazel Linden, Peggy and Wren are waiting in a restaurant. If Peggy doesn't show up after asking Wren to wait in the lobby, Peggy will go to the front desk and inquire as to whether anyone else has been looking for them.

Peggy takes Wren's hand as the concierge approaches, and the two of them cross the foyer. Standing in the restaurant lobby, Hazel and Kelty alternately look toward the elevators and the establishment. When a man and a woman come closer, Hazel looks for signs of Flora in the woman's face. Hazel waits for the tremor or knowing tingle that would let her know if this is her sister as they shake hands. Camellia, however, says it's not her as she emerges from the corner. Wren's sorrowful smile hints that Miss Linden had hoped Hazel would be her sibling. In front of the hotel, in the Victorian Embankment Gardens, and facing the River Thames, the group gathered.

The iron statue of Robert Burns was seated behind Hazel and Kelty, who were speaking to Camellia and facing Wren and Peggy. Peggy expressed regret for her sister's disappearance and questioned her mother's deception regarding Whisperwood. Peggy stepped forward and asked, "Mother, how did you come upon it?" She pointed at Wren, who was usually in danger. A woman with long ebony hair came up to them and yelled, "Peggy Maria Andrews, what have you done?" When Peggy Andrews arrives on a plane, Linda Andrews is taken aback.

The publishing house receives a letter from a crazy woman named Hazel Linden inviting her to visit England. Linda maintains that she sold a first edition of her book with original illustrations for them and for their future. Hazel accuses Linda of stalking, finding, and seducing her daughter.

Then, Hazel accuses Linda, Kelty, and Camellia of having spent her entire life searching for her daughter. Linda screams, but Camellia carries on, moving closer. Linda and Camellia are talking about the incident involving Flora, Hazel's sister, who was shot down in Pearl Harbor by the barbarians.Linda reveals that her aunt Maria told them the tale for a year and used it as a pacifier to calm herself.

Maria volunteered for a group that sent women overseas to assist with the children of war widows. Then Linda says that Maria never told her the little girl's name and that Linda didn't care. Linda Andrews and her daughter Hazel are talking about the tale Maria told them about a missing child. Maria is a young English girl. Linda says that although Maria assisted numerous families, this particular tale stayed with her and she believed it had saved the girl. After three years, Linda lost Maria, and this tale now belongs to her family as much as it does to theirs.

To find out if anyone will recognize the family or the young girl from Newcastle, Camellia suggests speaking with Dorothy Bellamy. A reporter named Dorothy Bellamy who wrote for "younger smarter women" was urged to speak with Hazel by her mother. Hazel quickly dialed the number after discovering a letter in the trash. She asked if she could meet the older woman in Binsey at The Perch in two hours after being startled to hear an older woman's voice. Journalist Dorothy Bellamy authored articles about kidnapped children.

Hazel hopes that her article will prompt someone to come forward with details about a young child who, in Newcastle, in 1940, spoke of a magical land.

Hazel is adamant about telling the truth in order to bring her sister back because Maria had taken the story to Cape Cod, Massachusetts. In London, Linda Andrews is with her mother Kelty, Peggy, and Wren.

The Perch in Binsey is a gleaming blue and silver establishment with an iron-scrolled table, two café cane chairs, and a small glass vase overflowing with two red roses. In the pleasantly warm midday sun, Hazel sat down and took off her red coat. She noticed Dorothy Bellamy entering the backyard and deduced that she was Flora's connection. Hazel's heart pounded with anticipation as she realized that her goal was to correct her error and set the world right. Hazel stood to face Dot as she made long strides toward the table.

Shadows from Dot's wide-brimmed hat fell across her face as she cast a glance around the garden lawn. She unbuckled her messenger bag and set a spiral-bound notebook on the table as she shook her head. She vowed to show the utmost respect for Hazel's sister. Hazel gets an uncanny sense of familiarity as she watches Dot Bellamy's red lips move while she speaks. She then notices Dot Bellamy's birthmark on her wrist, which resembles two splayed east-west rabbit ears.

Hazel is convinced that if she is born knowing, she will navigate the woods to the place that was created especially for her. She avoided Flora for a year, but now she finds herself in the unexpected presence of the journalist she avoided for a year. Sisters Dot and Hazel Bellamy have been looking for one another for twenty years. Hazel realizes Flora is in her arms when Dot says she is Dorothy May Bellamy. "You are not a dream. You are my sister," Dot cries, and they are both in each other's arms.

All of Hazel's previous fantasies pale in comparison to this instance of pure and unmerited grace. Hazel is holding the body of her now-grown sister as Dot and she stand in Binsey, England. Dot has been looking for Flora Lea Linden for the past two years because she is obsessed with her childhood memoir. She is now in possession of Dorothy May Bellamy, a person she had dreamed about. Dorothy May Bellamy was born in Newcastle, England, the daughter of Claire and William Bellamy, the sister of four brothers, and the cousin of numerous individuals. One necklace each for Hazel, the woman in the stone cottage, and Dot herself, for Flora, were created from the long, ower-strewn string that Dot's mind had combined into.

CHAPTER TEN

Dot's voice becomes softer, more innocent, and straightforward in its conviction. At The Perch, Dot and Hazel cross paths. Dot believes Flora Lea Linden drowned in the River Thames. The girl she's been looking for all this time is Dot, the River Child. Dot's mother has never stopped looking for Hazel's mother, who is still alive. Dot's mother claims she had vivid dreams involving a well, a hollow tree, and Dot's voice.

Childhood friends Hazel and Dot have been looking for each other their entire lives. Dot recalls a magical place called Whisperwood where she was instructed to transform into a certain person. Hazel tells Dot that even though her life had been kept a secret from her, it had always been there, waiting for her. Dot tries to push the image away, but it swoops up and suffocates her. Dot receives Hazel's assurance that she won't fail.

In Binsey, where Hazel and Dot first meet, Hazel learns Flora Lea Linden is still alive. They discuss their early years, the train to Oxfordshire, the woods, Harry's reading progress, the nurses who worked behind the rectory, and trips to the Oxford University Library.

Dot shook her head, but Hazel went on to explain the background of the Pauline Baynes illustrations and the Peggy Andrews book. Imogene, Dot's aunt, cautions her to steer clear of these accounts of the missing children. Imogene, a nurse in Binsey who worked there when they lived there, takes Dot.

The sound of a woman calling out interrupts Dot and Hazel, and they are also interrupted by Mum running into The Perch's backyard. Dot receives a hug from her mother, who also informs her that she has been located. Under the cover of the willow, Hazel joins her mother and sister and inquires as to how they can assist. Dot adjusts her hat so that a shadow covers her eyes before putting it back on her head. Dot and Hazel are two distinct individuals who are working to make up for their differences.

Hazel's mother collapses onto the café chair as Dot strolls across the lawn. After enjoying live music, gin zzes, and dancing at Ronnie Scott's Jazz Club in the West End, Peggy and Wren return to the hotel by foot. Peggy is overcome by it all, Wren's touch, and how much of the world she had missed while living in the tiny yellow house on the sand dune.

The most crucial information in this text is that Whisperwood's creator, who lived in Bloomsbury, London, left a phone number for Peggy. Peggy and Wren strolled the streets, window-shopped without making a purchase, relaxed in a coffee shop, and then went to a beauty salon where Peggy asked a male hairdresser to cut her hair in the style of Jackie Kennedy after showing him a magazine photo of the former first lady.

When Peggy and Wren arrived at The Savoy, Peggy took off her hat, letting her short hair brush against the collar of the sky blue coat Wren had given her the day before they visited the British Library. In a hotel lobby, Peggy and Wren come across their mother, Mother, who is seated on a chair with her hands folded in white gloves. When Peggy asks her mother if she is okay, she responds by warning her that there are dangers all around her. Mother sobs sincere tears of regret for what she has done to Peggy. Wren nods and extends a hand to Peggy.

Peggy looks around the lobby, which is deserted save for a single nighttime concierge wearing a tall black hat. Since this afternoon, Peggy has been residing with her mother, Mother. She and Wren are sharing a room, but tonight she will have a separate space.

Mother grants her forgiveness and informs Peggy that Flora has been located. Peggy is appreciative of her mother's generosity and love.

The morning after Dot Bellamy is found, Hazel wakes up with the idea of finding Flora. Her promise to give Kelty the evening to speak with the family and call Aiden Davies is made over the phone to Kelty. Kelty consents to allow Imogene some time to leave. While Barnaby is pictured standing in the kitchen doorway, Hazel imagines each of them clinging to the newly revealed and imperfectly understood story. Hazel chuckles at the irony as she notices how strongly he smells of cigarettes and late-night pub food.

Journalist Hazel has avoided Barnaby for the past 12 months. When Lord Arthur Dickson of Sotheby's calls to reassure her that her job is secure, she declines the job offer from Sotheby's. She is reminded of Poppy, who was homeless but was still hired by Edwin Hogan, and of Barnaby's father, who called on her behalf to establish her suitability. Hazel decides to turn down the position as her heartbeat quickens in her ears. A book and its illustrations helped Hazel Linden realize what she wanted out of life, and as a result, she declined her dream job.

Barnaby walks into the kitchen wearing a gray pair of pants and a white T-shirt. He asks her what's going on as he fixes his gaze on her. He refuses to take a bite of her egg and toast as she explains that she is both lost and found. He's attempting to decide what to do next. The most crucial information in this passage is that Hazel has been receptive to the truth and the freedom it brings, and that Barnaby has allowed her access to Whisperwood after she had stopped going there out of fear.

She thinks Flora was lost in the narrative, but in the interim, she left a significant portion of herself in those wooded areas. She should return to Whisperwood stronger, not weaker, as Barnaby sincerely regrets having hurt her. Barnaby and Hazel are talking about how they feel about one another. When Hazel was younger, she recalls kissing Harry and dispensing with her obligations. Hazel insists that her desire for Barnaby is insufficient when Barnaby asks if it is.

When he follows up by asking Hazel if she is free of the person she loved before him, she replies that she has been piling up boxes and bags in his attic for three years. Hazel responds that she has boxes and bags stacked up in his attic when he asks if she is free of the person she loved before him.

On March 20, 1960, Barnaby and Hazel show up at the Thames Valley Police Station in Henley-on-Thames. At the low white-picket gate, where Hazel has been waiting for him, Aiden Davies is waiting for them. Hazel is instructed by Aiden to call Aiden Davies and inform him of Imogene Wright's potential for killing Dot Mulroney.

Hazel tucks her chin deeper into her green wool scarf as she pulls it closer. Before putting on his police cap and nodding, Aiden raises it and rubs his head. When Dot Bellamy and Aiden Davies arrive at Dot's aunt's home, it has a thatch roof and is constructed of cream-colored stucco. Dot pulls a fleece-lined coat off the wall pegs, sags her shoulders into it, and slowly buttons it. A calico cat tried to escape while three dogs barked.

In the backyard of Imogene Mulroney's house, a concrete bench serves as a waiting area for Dot and Aiden. Dot looks perplexed while grinning sadly. The most crucial information in this passage is that Dot, Hazel's sister, was sent to Wallsend, a tiny community outside of Newcastle, in order to be reunited with her family. Dot had spoken with hundreds of evacuees, some of whom had tried hypnotherapy and said the procedure had permanently changed their lives.

When Aiden came back, Dot realized that Hazel was one of them as she and she waited for him.

As Hazel's suspicion increased, she paced the garden as Aiden burst through the gate, his face mottled and red. When Dot and Aiden learn that Aunt Imogene has vanished, they are horrified. Despite Dot and Aiden's best efforts, she is still there. Then Aiden reveals that Dorothy May Bellamy, now known as Flora Lea Linden, was taken by Mrs. Mulroney in order to save her life. When Dot and Aiden learn that Dorothy May Bellamy, now known as Flora Lea Linden, was taken by Mrs. Mulroney and saved from certain death, they are horrified.

Dot's mother was allowed to visit the country by Hazel's mother while Imogene saved Dot from a raging river. Imogene gave Flora to them to replace the daughter Dot's sister Claire had lost to consumption. Hazel nearly reached out to grab Imogene as she screamed at her for using her to replace a dead child. Hazel was unsure if Imogene actually spat at her feet. Hazel was so enraged that she was on the verge of grabbing Imogene with her hands.

The fact that Hazel saved Dot from drowning and then hid her in a church is the most crucial information in this text. She later brought her to Newcastle to take the place of her mother's deceased child, and Imogene later brought her there as well. The two then talk about how they kept Dot hidden in a church and why they decided against telling the police. Imogene then touches Dot's face once more after Dot explains that she was brought to Newcastle to replace a dead child of her mother's. The kidnapping of Flora Lea Linden on October 19, 1940, is a topic of conversation between Aiden and Hazel.

Aiden cautions Hazel that anything she does or says could be used as evidence despite her belief that Imogene Mulroney is currently in custody for the kidnapping. Then, after hearing Flora's cries, Hazel decides to make a vow to save Imogene and goes to the church in the middle of the night. Then, Aiden informs Hazel that Imogene Mulroney has been detained in connection with the kidnapping of Flora Lea Linden on October 19, 1940, and that failing to mention something that she might later use in court could hurt her defense. Aiden Davies dragging Imogene into a police car is seen by Hazel and Dot. Dot collapses to the bench as she senses the childish side of her slipping away behind the lies Imogene had thrown into the morning air.

Dot wonders why Imogene took her if she wasn't helping her, even though Hazel apologizes for leaving her alone. Dot thinks Imogene stole her because she loved her, but Hazel suppresses her own rage. Dot's parents never revealed to her that she was actually two people. Hazel was driven to convince Dot that Imogene's lies were dishonest, untrue, and tainted with egotistical madness. Dot lived a happy life, but the truth of her upbringing was a lie.

Dot's aunt has loved and cared for Flora her entire life despite the fact that she gave her what she believed God commanded. Hazel invites Dot to Binsey so that she can see Bridie because the pain of Flora possibly going missing once more overwhelms her. Dot shivered and zipped the gray wool around her neck as if she were trying to protect herself. Dot agrees to take Hazel to Binsey after Hazel tells her that they have an invisible place with them.

On the feast of St. Frideswide, Bridie, Hazel, Dot, and Harry reach the stone cottage where Imogene Wright has abducted Flora. Dot explains to Bridie that although she was once Flora, she is now Dorothy McCallister, married to Harry, and uses her maiden name as her byline.

While Harry's worn-out red VW van grinds down the driveway, Bridie and Dot enjoy a cup of tea as dust and pebbles rise like smoke. After 20 years apart, Harry Aberdeen and Dot Bellamy are evading their mother, Bridie. Harry gives Dot a cheek kiss and introduces her as Vanity Fair magazine's Dorothy Bellamy.

They discuss Flora, the woman they had known as children, as Harry cradles Dot in his arms. Bridie shrugged and said that up until this point, she had no idea why she needed Harry. Dot's cap was grabbed and held by Harry as he shook his head. Dot listened and observed as the individuals she was supposed to know joyfully discussed her return with one another. To confront Aunt Imogene, who has been detained and either had her childhood stolen from her or preserved, Dot Bellamy is in Henley-on-Thames.

She has never seen anything like what happened yesterday with Aunt Imogene, and her mind is disorganized. She finds a place to sit on a hay bale with Hazel, but she needs air and space. Harry smiles at her, and she finds a place to sit on a hay bale with Hazel. Dot Bellamy is a six-year-old girl living in Whisperwood, a magical land where she lives with her sister Berry.

She is awakened by an owl calling her name, Flora, and is taken to a starry river in her magical land of Whisperwood.When she wakes up, she is surprised to find that the water is made of stars and she is tumbling underwater, holding her breath until it burns. Harry and Hazel are present, and Dot remembers her sister calling her name. Dot and Harry Aberdeen are standing in the pasture land of Bridie and Harry Aberdeen when Dot is startled into the river by Aunt Imogene's voice.

She sways under the fevered dreams of being trapped in a small room, which are not from fairy tales or nightmares. Bridie explains that the magical land Hazel had kept hidden away for all these years had been working its magic, bringing them ever closer until this day when they stood in the pasture land of Bridie and Harry Aberdeen.

Dot speaks slowly and carefully, articulating every word she needs to hear. Bridie believes that Dot was given a white pill that tastes bitter and biting, and they both know that they did not lose her. The most important details in this text are that Flora Lea Linden was kidnapped by a nurse damaged from war, out of her mind, stalking and stealing a little girl.

Hazel believed her imagination and love for Harry had been the cause of her disappearance, but it wasn't her imagination or love for Harry that caused her to be kidnapped. Dot then threw her arms around Flora Lea Linden and held her close.

After the river, there is nothing but Newcastle, university, Russel and Connor, and then searching for the lost children of Pied Piper. Dot, Harry, Hazel, and Bridie are gathered around a table to discuss the story of Flora Lea Linden, a lost child who was taken to Newcastle by her aunt Imogene. Flora had been only a few hours away from London in a remote village with a different mother, and Dot understands why she did what she did. The story brings Dot back to her family, as she has been writing about the lost children of Pied Piper for years. Hazel and Dot are discussing the story of Kelty, a lost child found in America.Hazel is obsessed with writing about lost children, but her husband Russel is worried it takes her away from him and their four-year-old son, Connor. Dot remembers a woman named Maria who helped her mother and other mums during the war. Maria took the story back to America and told her sister, Linda, about it to help calm Peggy, who had also lost her father in the war.

Dot and Harry stand outside Bridie's home. The night was crisp and clear, the sky indigo with stars.

Hazel sensed Harry's body next to her, her longing for him as strong as that afternoon of the Feast of St. Frideswide when his kiss had made her forget all reason and responsibility. Harry spoke of a miracle, a young girl telling a story to an American volunteer who carries it across the sea for her niece. Hazel allowed the blessing of those words to fall over her, saying she never gave up on her belief that Flora could be found. Hazel and Harry have lost each other, but they still have a choice to make. Harry suggests that it is about having what is right now and not squandering what remains.

Hazel is ready to go to the station, and Harry kisses her on the cheek. She realizes that freedom has its own price, but she must be careful.Dot Bellamy discovered the truth of her past a week after her disappearance. She was visited by a psychiatrist who specializes in childhood trauma from the war, who told her how memories were blocked and how the mind holds that truth. Dot was trying to figure out if deception negated the honest parts of her life, and she was writing down scattered memories to build a cohesive story of the day of her disappearance.

Writing was the only way to make sense of the mad world she now found herself navigating. Dot's Vanity Fair editor, Mia Hardingham, anxiously awaited the article and Dot sewed together the torn pieces of both Hazel's and Imogene's retellings to fashion a cloth of story.

Dot had walked the paths of Binsey alone and entered St. Margaret's Well, which belonged to both St. Margaret and St. Frideswide. The church and the Anglican Church had given the chapel another name, but the essential nature of the sanctuary and the well remained. Dot allowed images and fear to rush over her, knowing they could not drown her. Dot and Flora are evacuees who are taken to a cottage by a nurse named Imogene. Imogene takes Flora from the river and carries her to the cottage where the four nurses live.

Flora tries to point to the cottage, but is bundled tight in a thick coat. Flora mumbles magical words to make Imogene turn and take Flora to Bridie, Hazel, and Harry, but instead they arrive at the cottage alone. Imogene sat Flora on a kitchen chair and pulled off Flora's wellies and dumped the water into the sink. Flora begs Imogene to take her home. Flora has been left alone by her family and has been searching for her sister in Whisperwood, a magical land.

Imogene, a nurse, returns with a woolen blanket and a white pill to make Flora feel better. Flora is carried across the cemetery to St. Margaret's church and the dark well where the princess Frideswide had once healed others. Imogene and Flora enter the tiniest room Flora has ever seen, with a window so small that the light coming through seemed like a lit lantern. Flora is taken to Whisperwood, a secret land where she betrayed her sister Hazel. The nurse sets her on a bench with a crucifix of Jesus and promises to return with dry clothes and warm food.

Flora shivers and falls in and out of half delirium until she falls into a fitful sleep. Later, Imogene returns with warm soft clothes that are not Flora's. The nurse dressed Flora and fed her a cup of warm potato soup. At the room's doorway, a flowered valise with leather handles awaits. Hazel, Dot, and Mum have spent the past days together building the lost structure of their lives: stories, bricks, and love.

Dot is struggling to reconcile the memories and love into something new, while Hazel is mourning Flora's loss. Dot is rebuilding her life, relearning the cornerstones of her childhood long lost.

Being with Dot and relearning the cornerstones of her childhood long lost has kept Hazel from dwelling too much on Barnaby. Hazel has spent many years worrying about who loved her and has forgotten to consider who she loves. She has almost gone twice in the past week to tell him she loves him, but she can't find a gentle place to settle in her heart.

She practices lines that don't ring true and goes to the kitchen for tea, toast, and an egg. She sets her notebook and Woolf pen on the kitchen table and turns on the baroque English wireless. She picks up where she left off the morning before she was headed to Paris with Barnaby. Hazel had a choice to leave for Paris or try one more time to discover the truth of the Whisperwood novel's origins. She decided to set her own words to paper and allow the story to break free from the sarcophagus of shame.

Late in the afternoon, she set her pen aside and took a long walk alone through Kensington Gardens. She arrived at Hogan's Rare Book Shoppe, where Tim and Poppy sat on stools behind the front desk. Hazel spied Edwin sitting at his ink-stained desk across from a young woman in a smart pale blue tweed suit. Edwin had a degree in English literature, making this shop a better fit for him.

CHAPTER ELEVEN

Hazel's arrival at Hogan's is an unforeseen happenstance that has altered the status of the job opening.Edwin recognizes her as an unforeseen happenstance and docks her check each month until she pays him back for any ruined or stolen merchandise. After an hour, Hazel returns to work with Tim, Edwin, Poppy, and rare books. She feels her life growing with every word she's written in her notebook, recounting the awful, beautiful, terrible, and enchanting days of Binsey. Hazel finds a parcel worth far more than she expected, and Edwin offers to draw two new original illustrations to replace the ruined ones and one extra to make the package even more worthwhile for a buyer.

Edwin hugs Hazel for the first time since she'd met him, and she reveals that Lord Arthur Dickson does not need or want to hear from her.After logging in the last box's contents, Hazel returns to the bookstore's main room, where Poppy and Tim stand behind the counter near the register. They close early. Hazel is looking for something rare and true in The Plough. Harry is looking for imagination and goodness, woodlands and magical creatures, and a river where stars owe to the sea.

Hazel has been on a quest to find Flora, but she has already made her decision in the riven hollow of an oak tree.

In March 1962, two years after the brown parchment package arrived at Hogan's Rare Book Shoppe, Hazel and Harry Aberdeen lived in the Celtic Sea of St. Ives in Cornwall. They have written a better ending and written a better ending for their daughter, Midge, who is now ten years old. They have opened a rare book and illustration studio on the Cornish coast, H2: Art, Books, and Original Illustrations, and have been working hard to open the gallery for two years. Hazel and Harry are proud of their daughter, Midge, but she knows it is far from fancy. She has lived with the dust and grime and the long backbreaking hours it took to open the gallery.

Harry and Hazel equal H2, and they combine their work and local art with rare books and their specialty: original illustrations from famous novels and fairy tales. Hazel steps down the worn eighteenth-century carved stone stairs to enter the main gallery, where she finds a hand-curated gallery of Pauline Baynes drawings from the Peggy Andrews Whisperwood collection, handmade jewelry, drawings, paintings, etchings, cushions, pottery, and a pile of books by Hazel Mersey Linden, The River Child: A Memoir of Whisperwood.

Hazel isn't sure her child is a girl, but she suspects they will name their child Flora Lea Aberdeen. Kelty places a hand on Hazel's stomach, asking if she is sure it's not twins. Kelty is proud of Hazel, who is setting up an art show and book signing in a seaside town.Harry is the best man she's ever met, and the gallery is full of patrons, friends, and family. Tenny has a date hanging on his arm, and Dot and her husband, Russel, and their son, Connor, stand together in front of the Baynes illustrations. Dot and Hazel are more than sisters now, and they have formed a new relationship out of long walks and leisurely teas. Peggy and Wren arrive at Harry and Hazel with hugs and kisses. It has been over a year since Book Two of Whisperwood sailed into England, and the publishing house sent Peggy to London for an extended book tour.

Hazel and Peggy share a deep connection, and Hazel forgives Linda for saving Imogene Wright. Bridie and Mr. Nolan arrive, and Hazel kisses her mother-in-law and takes Mr. Nolan's hand. They are not leaving until after Hazel has had her baby. Bridie, Aiden Davies, friends from St. Ives, other artists, shop owners, and tourists are all attending the grand opening of H2 and Hazel's book signing. Hazel's literary agent Meg bursts through the door with a smile.

Harry climbs onto a wooden platform and clinks his crystal with a toast. The room hushes until it is quiet enough for Harry to continue. Hazel loves Dot and her return, and she opens a place in St. Ives. She tells Dot that the Celts speak of thin places, and that the land is liminal, transporting, and mystical. She tells Dot that the Celts speak of thin places, and that every package that arrives here could be an adventure, quest, or mystery. She hopes that everyone will find the land made just for them in an unmapped realm in their souls.

Made in the USA
Monee, IL
10 November 2023